I0430037

The Income Investor

"Give yourself a raise every month."

The Income Investor

"Give yourself a raise every month."

George R. Sealy

The Income Investor

"Give yourself a raise every month."

Copyright   George R. Sealy

Published by Pensarz LLC
1238 W. Harding Ave.
Coolidge, AZ 85128
USA
http://pensarz.media

All rights reserved. No part of this book may be reproduced, scanned, or distributed in any printed or electric form without permission.

Cover and inside image: katjen/shutterstock.com
License fee paid

FIRST EDITION

ISBN: 9798884115828
Imprint: Independently published

Disclaimer

In this book, I mention specific stocks from time to time for data and case study examples. However, that reference should never be confused with recommending a stock for investing. Nothing is ever static in the stock market. Market conditions change by the minute. Investors should always do appropriate analysis and take action based on current market conditions. **Stocks purchased and sold are the sole responsibility of the investor.** Specifically, neither the author nor Pensarz, LLC are liable for investor losses. Past performance and examples presented in this book are NOT predictors of future success.

Along the way, I mention Charles Schwab as my financial backbone, transaction base, and brokerage tool. I receive absolutely no funds from Charles Schwab for my endorsement. I refer to them solely because they have provided a highly professional and complete framework on which to grow my wealth and income. From time to time, I reference the services they provide. If a person wants to use another brokerage service, my comments can be used as a basis for comparison.

Contents

THE INCOME INVESTOR

Forward

Hello, I hope your life is going well. There is a good chance that it will get even better after reading this book. You have arrived at a good place.

I began planning this book in 2019. Little did anybody foresee the events in the years 2020 through 2022. The pandemic created world-wide repercussions. Not only did millions of people die, but there was significant financial destruction. In 2019, I was making invest-ments, generating income, and making plans for the coming months. Suddenly in early 2020, everything turned upside down. The econ-omy came to a standstill. People stopped working. Restaurants closed. People didn't travel. The federal government sent checks to millions of people. Interest rates plummeted to near zero. As the months rolled along, we saw inflation rise to over 9% with fuel and food prices striking the heart of people's bank accounts. Mortgage rates hit 40-year highs. Credit card balances ballooned as people needed to buy staples just to live.

In 2023, The US Federal Reserve attacked inflation by raising inter-est rates, thereby attempting to quash consumer demand. It has worked to a degree as inflation has eased off. In early 2024, the economy is gradually returning to normalcy. People have returned to work. The forecast is for the Federal Reserve to begin lowering in-terest rates in the second half of 2024. The stock market has re-bounded to all-time highs.

The events of the past four years have served to reinforce my belief in the system that I have used to improve my financial well-being. While those four years were daunting I came through it just fine. However, I did change my perspective of how I wanted to position this book. In 2019, I just wanted to show people various investment avenues to create more income. I planned to comment on each of them and how to gauge what they could do. Then I realized that much of my success has to do with the *process* that I use. And I believe that my *process* is somewhat unique and very effective. So, I have expanded the book to include both process steps and investment perspectives. It is a powerful combination.

This book should be especially helpful to young people who want to get on a solid, long-term financial path. Many young people know they should save or invest, but they go at it on an intermittent basis. Every so often they put money in a savings account. Or knowing something about the stock market, they buy securities on a hunch or based on a friend's recommendation of a hot stock. Or maybe they feel that participating in their company's 401K plan is all they need for their future.

Older people will also benefit from this book. Those of you in this category will like the structure and disciplined approach. It will fit with the mature outlook you have come to know. Thereby it will feel comfortable, logical, and rational. It will help supplement income from Social Security, pension plans, and annuities.

The *process* that one uses is as important as the investments one makes.

This book focuses on creating income apart from that which is earned from employment. Having a good, well-paying job is the first step to having a happy and successful adult life. With a job, you can buy a car, a house, furniture, go on vacation, and so on. Those are wonderful things. However, there is a next step in the process, which is to garner income beyond regular employment income. The common term for this is **passive income**. This concept will become clear as we work through the various means to accomplish it.

There are many ways to achieve a growing and persistent passive income. This book discusses a subset of those. The idea is to give you a toolset and the insight to create a significant passive income that grows over time. Given that knowledge, you should be able to determine what is the best path to follow. Then you can then go about creating a plan and executing it. The great thing is that you will be taking an active interest in YOUR money management. That is exactly what everyone should do.

This book presents a little different perspective on stock market investing compared to what most people discuss. It is what I call, "Income Investing." Income Investing is not discussed very much on television or cable financial television/Internet channels. I would say the reason is that it is not very exciting for a lot of people. Therefore, it doesn't get the buzz that is associated with other kinds of investing. However, I have found that it works well. One reason is that it uses solid financial analysis principles and has the right metrics in place. It is rooted in solid financial concepts as opposed to hype and fluff opinion. It is a solid framework for success.

Income investing is a long-term strategy. It is for people who want to base their future on solid foundations as opposed to quick get-rich hysteria. It takes time and patience, but it works.

So let us get started on the road to a more financially secure future. It will be worth it.

Good luck to you,

George R. Sealy

February 2024

1

How to Think About Your Money

The first thing to grasp is how to think about your money. Let's write that again: YOUR MONEY. You work hard for your money, at least 40 hours a week. Some people work 60-hour weeks including weekends. Their jobs demand that kind of commitment. To get that money, you might have to deal with pressure, deadlines, customers, and management that wants more and faster.

With that in mind, comes the first and most important rule you will ever learn:

Rule 1: If you are not concerned about your money, don't expect anyone else to be.

I have seen many people work hard and make good money, and then not take care of what they have earned. They get frivolous with their money, get deep in debt, and fail to plan for their future. Some people trust other people with their money. They assume their money will be well invested. It's amazing how some people only have a general notion of how much they spend on gasoline, food, and utilities each month. It seems as though they believe there is an invisible hand or magical genie who will take care of them as long as they work hard. It isn't so. What does happen is that they fail to do as well as they could. They might even get into financial distress.

YOU must take an active interest in your financial health and plan for the future. No one will do it for you. Even financial planners will not care as much about you as you do or should. Therefore, just about every day you should take stock of where you are and what you are going to do. It doesn't have to take a long time, but it's like locking your front door at night. It's just something that you do. It is not that you are worried about your money, instead, it is that you are *managing your money*.

So, as a first rule, **take a very active interest in managing your money**. Do not assume that because you are working in a job everything will be fine regardless of what you do. That is not necessarily the case. Furthermore, making good decisions, as opposed to no decisions, can result in enormous beneficial rewards in the future. Small, good decisions add up and thereby multiply their impact. If those decisions are not made, then the multiplicative effect is lost. The earlier you can be actively involved with managing your money, the better off you will be.

Managing your money does NOT mean you are a miser. That is, you are not the old, greedy guy counting his gold coins every day. You are not the person who hoards money only to look at it and be happy with what you gathered. More so, because you are actively managing your money, then you know that you can confidently purchase and engage in those things in life that give you happiness. You know that you are comfortable with what you are doing, and that alone makes it even sweeter. It is a perfect place to be.

Let's conclude this chapter by repeating the first rule:

Rule 1: If you are not concerned about your money, don't expect anyone else to be.

Live it every day.

2

The Process Mindset

Before Henry Ford appeared, automobile manufacturers built cars one at a time. It was a laborious, time-consuming process in which an employee had to learn many skills. Naturally, they would be better in some skills compared to others. They would also be slower or faster in completing tasks. There was little consistency. It was Ford's genius to change the model. He created the assembly line wherein an employee learned one skill and repeated it over and over. Accordingly, the employee's task completion speed also improved. Henry Ford's process produced cars faster and better. Henry Ford became exceptionally wealthy. His legacy continues today. While there are concerns about meaningful work it is the concept of consistency that we are discussing here.

Is there a process for teaching children at school? Yes. Children are bussed or travel to a central location where they can be taught efficiently by a teacher in a classroom with lots of resources. They are divided into groups by age, and they are taught subjects appropriate for their intellect at their stage of development. Then they go home. The process continues day after day as they progress through the grade levels. It is organized and productive. Parents, teachers, children, the administration, and the public know what to expect. We have moved into an age of cyber school that alters the process, but it is still a process.

Is there a process for departing and returning planes at an airport? Yes. Pilots of planes have to file a flight plan. They communicate with the airport tower to be cleared for takeoff. On nearing arrival, pilots communicate with the airport tower to land the plane. If there were no process, then there would be chaos at airports with planes colliding and worse. This process is repeated hundreds of times a day at a given airport, and thousands of times a day across the US. Everyone involved completely understands the protocol, and a problem rarely occurs.

The point is that **an appropriate process improves results.** It helps to eliminate inefficiencies. It helps to avoid problems and chaos. A solid, well-constructed process can be used over and over, like Ford's assembly line, to produce extraordinary outcomes.

However, many people fail to use good processes in their personal lives. This is very much true with investing and creating income. Some people put money in a savings account every so often "for a rainy day." Some people have paycheck money placed in a 401K and forget about it until the next yearly statement. Other people hear of a hot stock from a friend, invest in it, and then hope for a home run return. Other people, let a third party make investment decisions by saying such things as "He knows all about that. I trust him." The point is many people don't work at investing as a process that is repeated over and over. It is an afterthought. And yet, other than family health and well-being, income and wealth management are some of the most important things a person can do. It makes the difference between living well or just getting by and moving into living better.

This book talks a lot about investment processes, which could be surprising to people. They are not theories. On the contrary, they are processes that have worked well over decades through all kinds of US and worldwide financial conditions.

Accordingly, here is the second important rule:

Rule 2: Adopt solid investment processes, and use them over and over.

3

Tools

There are three basic tools required to be able to implement the processes discussed in this book. They are a calculator, a spreadsheet program, and a brokerage account.

Basic Calculator

From time to time, it's necessary to use a basic calculator. That is, you need to be able to add, subtract, multiply, and divide. For example, you might want to determine how many shares of a given stock you can buy with the money you have. So, you would divide the money you have by the current price of the stock to determine the number of shares. As another example, you might want to calculate the return on investment you are about to make. In another case, you might want to determine which of several investment alternatives is the best. For these purposes, a simple calculator will do just fine.

All smartphones have a calculator program as part of the basic set of features. Microsoft Windows has a basic calculator program. Therefore, chances are you don't need to look for one.

The next step up is a *financial calculator*. These calculators allow one to determine such things as the future worth of a present value,

the future value of an annuity, or net present values. An example calculation would be to calculate the monthly mortgage payments of
loans given the amount of the loan, the number of payments, and the
interest rate. It takes a little bit of coursework to understand financial calculations. However, it is well worth it because you will gain a
greater understanding of how interest rates work and the time value
of money. You can do better investment analysis. There are many
books and publicly available videos to provide this information. You
don't need to learn financial analysis, but it adds a lot to one's maturity in financial management. Financial calculators are great and fun
to use. Spreadsheet programs also have financial calculator functions as part of the standard package.

Spreadsheet Program

A spreadsheet program such as *Microsoft Excel* is a required tool for
financial management. It provides a locus around which to focus
and plan for the future. When you open a spreadsheet program your
data is in front of you, and you are instantly working on improving
your financial situation.

In this book, spreadsheet programs are used for three purposes:
tracking, financial calculations, and goal setting. First of all, you
will want to track every investment you make whether they are cer-
tificates of deposits, stocks, or options. You will want to forecast the
income they will make for you. This should be tracked by the
quarter of each year, so that year over year you can see improvement.
Keeping these spreadsheets will provide a reference point. Simple
tracking of progress is a **major step** forward to improved financial
progress. The reason is that you will be actively engaged in your future. This is completely different than passively reviewing a
quarterly or yearly statement from an investment institution. When
you are sensitized to your income periodically, then you are more apt
to get involved to make things better. And that directly is in agreement with **Rule 1**.

 Second, spreadsheets do arithmetic calculations well. They allow
changes in one area to flow seamlessly to other areas so that you can
see the overall impact. For example, an investment in the first

quarter of a year will affect the second, third, and fourth quarter's forecasted income, and so forth. The dynamic capability of spreadsheets allows you to consider different investment alternatives quickly and efficiently. For example, you can determine whether it is better to buy a one-year CD or a stock that will make a return at a point in time. Again, you will be actively engaged in your future.

Third, and perhaps most important, is that you can set **financial goals** for the year and monitor progress regarding those goals as time passes. Spreadsheet programs provide a great means to set goals quarter by quarter and to summarize the goals for the year. They also provide means to compare actual performance with the goals. You will know exactly where you are at all times. And again, you will be actively engaged in the process.

Setting and tracking goals is an essential part of the process discussed in this book. Setting goals is very, very important because otherwise, you have no direction. Comparing actual numbers to goals gives feedback on successes and failures. You can understand what worked and what didn't. That is valuable information for an aspiring investor. Setting goals is detailed later in this book.

Rule 3: Set financial goals and work to achieve them.

I mentioned *Microsoft Excel* as a possible spreadsheet program. There are others. There are even spreadsheet programs available for smartphones. I like to see a lot of the spreadsheet within a single field of view. Therefore, spreadsheets work best for me on a personal computer using a big monitor. But that is certainly a personal preference.

Examples of spreadsheets are provided later. You will want to use these examples as a starting point and then tailor them to your needs.

Brokerage Account

The third tool you need is to have a brokerage account with a major service provider. This book is about making an income through investments. You need a means of doing that. I happen to use Charles Schwab, but there are several others. A brokerage account allows you to buy and sell securities in various markets. Such an account allows you to have direct control over your future as opposed to someone else doing it for you. And here I again refer to **Rule 1:If you are not concerned about your money, don't expect anyone else to be.**

Here are some features that I find important for a brokerage account:

- Access to direct buying and selling of many different types of securities: stocks, CDs, mutual funds, and options using secure Internet connections.

- Low transaction fees for buying and selling securities.

- Excellent year-end and interim reporting and forms, such as 1099s. These reports should be downloadable in digital form so they can be sent to tax accountants.

- Access to stock analysis reports from reputable and expert sources.

- Investment tools such as stock screeners that support numerous criteria filters.

- Ability to have numerous accounts such as Individual Retirement Accounts (IRAs), Roth IRAs, rollover IRAs, and a main brokerage account.

- Ability to talk about complex issues with highly intelligent and responsible account representatives. Sometimes the invested companies will perform complex financial maneuvers that show up in the brokerage account log. Expert interpretation might be required. It's nice to have someone to discuss these with highly knowledgeable people.

- Absolute security of your financial and personal information.

Additional features, I like:

- Ability to receive direct payments such as W2 payroll amounts. Or wire transfers from external sources.

- Ability to make payments, such as for bills, electronically or by check.

- Ability to track history and understand stock gains/losses, so that good decisions can be made.

- In particular I like Charles Schwab because they never "push" stocks, yet they are always available to answer questions. They never call to sell a stock. They do provide optional seminars and ideas. They have a mailed periodical that has many solid ideas and valuable information.

Charles Schwab is one investment company. There are others. You will need to do some research on financial deposit requirements for opening a brokerage account. They vary by company. It is best to do research and get the best fit for you.

A Different Process Approach

A good brokerage account can be a framework for organizing one's financial health and supporting daily transactions. I found that to be the case some forty years ago. I completely changed my orientation by having my paycheck directly deposited into my brokerage account. I paid bills from my brokerage account, and then I invested any excess funds remaining at the end of the month. Then I started the next month all over. This structure became transformational because instead of investing as an afterthought, it was integrated into my basic financial process. Again, I was always engaged in my financial health. I didn't have to spend a second depositing money for investment because it was already there. I suggest people to do it this way. It is the most efficient means to handle one's finances.

Summary

So now you have the essential tools for managing your financial wealth and income. You have the calculator, a spreadsheet program, and a brokerage account.

4

Basic Concepts

This book, 'The Income Investor,' is about creating a sustainable, consistent, and growing income stream outside of the workplace. Achieving that goal means a person is on the road to becoming more independent. It means that there are additional funds to pay bills, take vacations, and retire more comfortably. The ideas presented in this book are not new to the financial world. The application of those ideas is the result of some forty years of investing experience. However, for a lot of people, the perspective is unique. The book gathers several ideas and strategies together to make things more comprehensive. At the end of the book, you should have a firm idea as to what to do to work toward that goal.

The biggest contribution this book makes is emphasizing that active engagement and process are extremely important to success. Many people fail in this area. It doesn't take hours and hours of work to be successful. However, it takes regular and purposeful attention. It is about adhering to a process. Again, it is a mindset.

 Fundamentally The Income Investor wants real, new, tangible money to flow into financial accounts month after month, year after year. The Income Investor loves to say, "I am getting paid today." And the more often that happens, the better it is. It's a great feeling that at least part of a car payment is being made or that the electric bill is handled for the month by something other than employment income. As time goes by, more and more items are handled in this fashion. Life gets easier and easier. And hopefully, someday, a person might not need to work at all.

Income Investing versus Wealth Investing and Others

'Income Investing' focuses on creating a periodic, increasing income stream. There are many ways to do it. There are alternative financial instruments that can be used. The goal at this point is to arrive at common terminology and ideas.

For stock market-related 'Income Investing,' the expectation is for companies to deliver a stream of income from dividends. For this to happen, a company's earnings are of utmost importance. That is, a company's profitability is critical. The reason is that dividends are paid out of profits. The stock price might fluctuate within a range, but so long as the company is increasingly profitable, variations in the stock price are of secondary consequence to the Income Investor. Some companies have a many-year record of delivering and growing dividend payments. This is exactly the kind of performance an Income Investor wants. It very well could be a good thing if the stock price goes down. The reason is that the Income Investor could use the opportunity to buy more stock and thereby increase dividend income.

'Wealth Investing' is about accumulating stock and gaining wealth as the price of the stock goes up. The wealth investor is very much concerned about daily fluctuations in stock prices. Total wealth increases when stock prices rise, and total wealth decreases when stock prices fall. The wealth investor buys and sells stocks to preserve wealth or take advantage of opportunities when stock prices have fallen. Income production is secondary, and not the focus of the wealth investor. Many stocks in a wealth investor's portfolio might not even produce dividend income. 'Wealth Investing' usually has at least a several-month time frame. Traders look for favorable market conditions to buy stocks and then sell stocks when conditions are unfavorable. Market timing is important.

'Day Traders' buy and sell stocks on an hourly and daily basis. They try to take advantage of small stock market price changes. It is about making daily profits and accumulating cash for the next market play. Day traders intensely watch market trends. They follow the news closely looking for anything significant. They are into a stock and then out of that stock over short periods. Quite often they will 'cash out' at the end of the day just so they are not vulnerable to overnight news and the consequences thereof. Day traders may make arbitrage moves (buying in one market and selling in another market) just to gain a small advantage.

Most people and the media are generally into 'Wealth Investing.' The focus is on what the stock price will do over months and years. The media, such as CNBC and Fox Business, report on stock prices for a given day trying to make sense of news developments. They give company news and how that reflects on stock prices. Company earnings and revenue reporting are discussed concerning stock prices. Federal Reserve actions can greatly affect stock market prices. Individuals usually look at how stocks are doing in their IRA or brokerage account with a focus on the stock price. A person's collection of stocks, their portfolio, sums up to total wealth. Naturally, people want their total wealth to increase.

Is 'Income Investing' or 'Wealth Investing' a better focus than the other? The answer is no. It depends on what a person's goals are. And the two types of investing are not mutually exclusive. The Income Investor is likely to gain wealth even though the focus is on income. And the Wealth Investor is likely to generate income even though they don't think about it much. As we go through this book, I discuss the differences in more detail. However, in this book, our goal is increasing income. For now, just understand that income investing and wealth investing are two different views of the same world. We are not going to mention 'Day Trading' further as it is a completely different style and scope of making money using stock markets.

Fundamental Definitions

Just to provide a common understanding of concepts, here are a couple of definitions. I start very simply. You may know and understand these concepts. But it is suggested that you still read this section because there are a few wrinkles to grasp. And I want everyone to have a common understanding of the terms that are used later in the book. That will eliminate confusion. So, please take a few minutes to read over the definitions and make sure there is a clear understanding.

Investment or Investing: to put money to use, by purchase or expenditure, in something offering potentially profitable money back.

The two important things are that first, you are doing something with money and second, you expect to gain a ***profitable amount of money back from your activity***. Is buying a car an investment? Maybe no and maybe yes. If you buy a car for personal use, then the answer is no. The reason is that the car is just being used as a means of transport. You are just spending money on something that you want. But if you buy a car at a great price with the idea that you are going to resell it for more money than you paid for it, then the answer is yes. In this case, you are speculating that your money was well spent and the result will be more money than when you started once you bought and sold the car. Is buying a fancy, expensive camera an investment? Again, the answer is yes or no. If you are just going to take pictures of the family cat, then the answer is no. If you are taking wedding photos for money as part of a business, then the answer is yes. The point is that not all cases of spending money are investments. Many people use the term 'investment' loosely. Many times, they call it an 'investment,' but all they are doing is spending money.

Return: This is the extra money that you receive from your investment. If you invest $100 and make $10 so that you now have $110, then the return is $10. Returns are designated as positive or negative. A positive return means a profitable investment was made, and a negative return is a loss of money. So, when investing you expect a positive return. Return is also graded on the percentage of initial investment. For example, a 10% return means that the money received back is 1.1 times the amount of the initial investment. For example, if a person invested $1,000 and received $1,100 back, then they had a return of $100 or 10%.

Annualized Return: There is also the convention of grading a given return over one year. And so, it is called an 'annualized return.' This helps to compare returns over different timeframes. For example, suppose the $100 above was made in six months, then the 'annualized return' is 20%. That is, a 10% return was made in only one-half of a year. Suppose another person invested $1,000, but they made $125 in nine months. Their annualized return is 16.67%. The point is that while the first person's actual return in dollars was less, they had a better, annualized return. Comparing returns across different alternatives is an important aspect and concept of successful investing. I use 'annualized return' in many examples and case studies. Again, it is an important tool to use when making comparisons of different returns over different time frames.

Risk: This has to do with the possibility that the investment money you are putting to use can be completely lost. Risk can be anywhere from zero, that is no risk and the investment is completely safe, to extremely high, where there is a good chance that all investment money can be lost. Risk and return are related. Low risk usually means low returns. High risk usually means high returns, if they happen. An investor should always evaluate risk and return, and then decide what to do next. Some people cannot afford to lose any kind of investment, so they should invest in very low-risk situations. They should accept that returns will be minimal. Other people can easily afford to lose investments and they want to go after high-risk and high return situations. Everyone is different. Many times, people underestimate or miscalculate the amount of risk involved with a given investment. It results in an unrecoverable situation.

Income: In general, income is new money or funds flowing into a person's accounts. For example, when you work at a job you earn an income. You get paid for the hours and effort you make. It is brand new money that you never had before. You can also gain income from profitable investments. You can lose income too from poor investments. Income and return are not the same thing. A return is always about a specific investment, such as making a 7% return. Income is just a single number, either gained or lost. Our goal is to increase income every month and year by making the best possible investments.

Passive Income: In this book, passive income is income that is gained from no work at all. It is income that is generated from investments. Specifically, it excludes income from a job, a contract, or even money made at a swap meet. It's money that you will get even if you are sitting at home watching TV in your padded lounge chair. I also call it actual or real income because it is the type of income everyone should aspire to have. It is a measure of how you are doing income-wise. This perspective changes how people should view their situation. If you are making $100,000 a year, what is your real income? For many people, the answer is zero. The reason is that it all comes from job salary. So, if they are laid off or their company goes out of business, their total income goes with it. They are in a difficult situation. But suppose they made $20,000 a year in passive income? That money is coming whether they have a job or not, and it will help them to adjust and get another job. The situation is not as dire because some funds are arriving. The bottom line is that people should work to develop real income. That is where a person stands. Having a high-paying job is great, but companies have ups and downs just like people do. So, the goal should be to generate as much real or passive income as possible.

Taxable Income: This is income that is subject to state and/or federal taxes. It is reported on a tax return. Not all income is taxable either at the state and/or the federal level. Tax implications are always relevant and they impact Income Investors differently than they do Wealth Investors. We'll point out the differences as we go along. Sometimes tax implications make the difference between going one way or another way as far as the next steps in the investing process.

When a stock increases in value, is that real income? The answer is no. It is not any kind of income. So, if a person has $100,000 of stock and it increases to $150,000 in a year, they did NOT have an income of $50,000 that year. Their total wealth increased by

$50,000, but they did not have an income of $50,000. Assuming the stock remains in the account (not sold) the IRS will not tax that increase. When the stock is sold, then capital gains taxes come into play.

On the other hand, if a stock generates dividends of $20,000, then probably that amount is taxable to some degree. There are many different kinds of 'dividends' that are taxable or not taxable under different federal and state rules.

Inflation: Inflation is the increase in the cost of goods and services year over year. If inflation is 3% it means that the cost of goods is 3% higher than in the previous year. People notice inflation the most when they go to the grocery store or gas station. It is reported every month by the US government. There are a few different variants as to how it is calculated, but the concept is the same. The historical and current inflation numbers are easily found on the Internet.

A huge reason for active income investing is the desire to offset the effects of inflation. As a general benchmark, the goal is for the annualized percentage return on investment to be equal to or greater than the inflation percentage. This means that the buying power of the underlying investment will be unchanged. For example, suppose we have initially $1,000 to buy food. With 3% inflation, it will take $1,030 to buy the same food a year later. And let us not forget that inflation compounds because it is computed with respect to the prior year. At 3% inflation, the following year will require $1,060.90 to buy the same goods.

So, with all that said and understood, you are off and running. I hope these fundamental ideas are clear. Keep learning new concepts, and here is another rule:

Rule 4: Learn financial terminology. Be able to understand what is being said on business network programs.

5

The Savings Account

In Part II, I discuss specific Income Investor instruments for creating passive income streams. Some topics are easy requiring little text. Others are more complex. All of them are important. The comments provided are based on personal observations and experience. Quite possibly you will get a little different perspective on each of them and how they could fit into your income investing strategies.

The Savings Account

The savings account is the most basic income-producing alternative. Most people are familiar with it. The concept is to put some money away when needed, maybe for an emergency, at a later time. Money can be put into and taken from a savings account at any time.

Savings accounts generate income at a very modest interest rate. From the bank's point of view, a savings account is a source of cash for their use. However, the bank does not know when the funds will be withdrawn by the account holder. Banks must maintain a certain percentage level of cash to cover customer withdrawals. However, banks do not have to have 100% of the cash in savings deposits at all times. They can use the non-coverage amount for other purposes to generate income for them and to keep the bank in business. Banks are strictly governed by the US government to protect account holders.

Savings accounts have the lowest interest rates of the options discussed in this book. The actual rates can vary by the week or month. Bank savings accounts often have a monthly charge associated with them. Savings accounts having modest amounts might not generate enough interest to cover the monthly charge. Therefore, the savings account becomes a losing proposition even though the saver has the best intentions. People using savings accounts should be knowledgeable of monthly account charges, which should appear on the monthly statement.

As an Income Investor, the goal of the savings account should be viewed as a temporary accumulation area for funds to be used for investing at a later time. **Savings account interest rates are usually less than current inflation rates.** Therefore, hoarding money in a savings account for the long term is counterproductive. Effective buying or bill-paying power is decreased. The Income Investor wants to make bill paying easier.

Earlier in this book I mentioned that decades ago I changed my financial management strategy so that ALL of my monthly working wages were deposited into my Charles Schwab account. I closed my savings account. I maintained a checking account only to facilitate cash deposits and withdrawals using the bank's automated teller machines (ATMs), which are located everywhere. Checking account funds are very modest because I don't have many cash transactions. I continue to maintain this structure.

My Charles Schwab brokerage account functions as both a checking account and a savings account. They pay monthly interest on the cash in the account. I have no monthly fees. I can use their 'bill pay' system to pay bills automatically or under specific directions. Everything is tracked.

The biggest benefit of using the Charles Schwab account in this manner is that it has eliminated the step of putting money in a savings account or transferring money from the checking account into the brokerage account. I have monthly checks from various sources deposited directly. I always have funds available for investment purposes. It is very efficient and it saves valuable time. It allows me to focus on other things.

Charles Schwab is not the only company to provide such services. I am fairly certain that Fidelity does as well. There must be others. Charles Schwab happens to be the company I selected decades ago. I strongly encourage each person to do their own investigations and due diligence should they want to pursue a similar strategy. Learn the various features a company offers. Learn the investments required to open and maintain an account.

Rule 5: The Income Investor should view savings accounts as temporary holding bins to accumulate funds for future investments.

Process Suggestion: Set up a monthly amount for savings account deposits. Never fail to make the deposit. Accumulate money for investment as fast as possible. Otherwise, have an account, such as a brokerage account, where money is automatically deposited and accumulated.

6

Certificates of Deposit

A Certificate of Deposit (CD) is a promissory note, that is, a written promise to pay at a future time a sum of money. CDs are issued by banks to their customers. CDs are composed of three parts:

- The CD purchase amount in even one thousand increments, such as a $2,000, $5000, or $100,000 CD.

- The maturity date is the date when the bank will pay the future sum of money, which is the CD face value plus interest.

- The annualized percentage interest rate (APR) used to calculate the interest paid over the time frame of the CD. Probably 90% of CDs pay the interest when the CD matures. However, some CDs pay monthly and some pay semi-annually.

Customers purchase CDs from banks by giving the bank cash with the promise that the bank will return the cash plus interest on a specified date in the written agreement. An example is a $10,000 6-month CD with an APR of 5%. The CD is purchased for $10,000. Six months later the bank will pay the customer $10,250. The interest of $250 is equal to 5% of $10,000 divided by two because it is a 6-

month CD. Remember that CD interest rates are annualized. They are annualized so that various CDs over various maturity timeframes can be compared.

While it seems to the customer CDs are savings instruments, they are cash loans to the bank. The bank ties up the customer's cash for a specified and certain timeframe. This allows the bank to use that money to generate revenue above the interest to be paid to the CD customer. For example, the bank can issue car loans and mortgages, or provide credit card support all at rates exceeding the CD rate. Generally speaking, banks are happy to issue CDs because they know they can earn profits above the interest to be paid.

CD rates vary by the day, by the week, and by the month. In 2020, CD rates fell to near zero when the Covid-19 pandemic struck. However, inflation soared in 2021 and so did interest rates in 2022 as the Federal Reserve Bank took action. Interest rates peaked in late 2023 and slightly lowered in early 2024. The Federal Reserve Bank could lower their interest rates in 2024, whereupon CD interest rates will fall too. The current 30-year fixed rate mortgage is 6.88%. Credit card rates are in the 23% range. The current one-year CD rate is about 4.9%. We can easily understand why banks are happy to issue CDs. They always have a profit margin.

The Yield Curve

There is always a relation between the maturity length of the CD and the APR being offered. This is called the yield curve if one were to plot the data. Generally speaking, the interest rate should rise as the maturity length increases. The reason is that risk increases when it takes longer for the bank to pay off the loan. Additionally, banks are very happy to tie up a person's cash for long periods. They want to induce customers into longer-term CDs by offering higher interest rates. They can do more with the cash and it stabilizes the bank.

For example, here is a normal yield curve:

Length of CD	APR
3-month	3%
6-month	3.1%
9-month	3.2%
1-year	3.5%
2-year	3.7%
5-year	4.0%

This looks as follows —

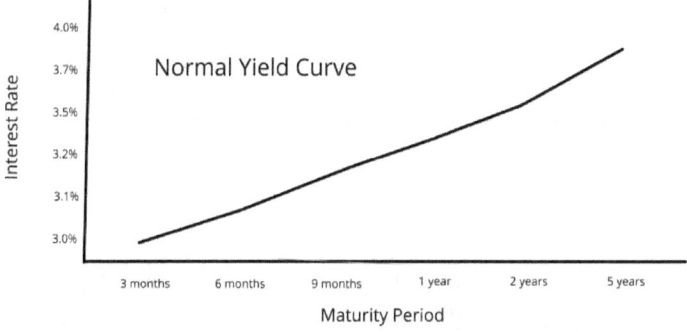

However, here is the actual yield curve data in early 2024:

Length of CD	APR
3-Month	5.251%
6-Month	5.216%
9-Month	5.030%
1-year	4.903%
2-Year	4.500%
5-year	4.100%

You can see that interest rates decline as the CD maturity term increases. This is called an *inverted yield curve*. TV business pundits will say, "This is a sure sign of an impending recession!" It remains to be seen, of course. So far, the Federal Reserve has avoided the so-called "hard landing" in dealing with inflation as they have raised interest rates over the last two years.

What it looks like. You can see that it is the opposite of a normal yield curve, and therefore it is *inverted*.

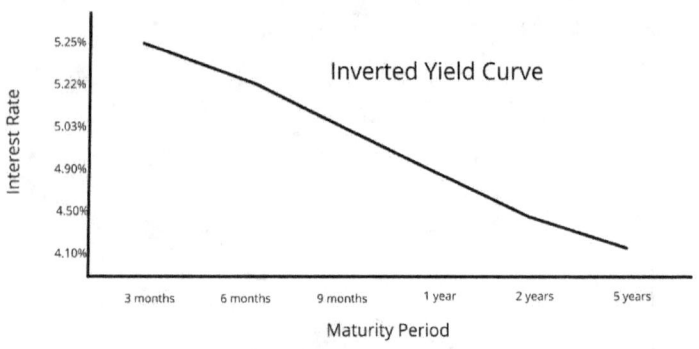

What is currently happening is that banks believe that Federal Reserve interest rates will fall over the long term. They are happy to pay high interest rates in the short term to acquire cash. But they don't want to be in a losing position long-term. They don't want to pay high-interest rates when the Federal Reserve interest rates have fallen. So, they are being cautious.

CD rates and the yield curve change daily. Nothing is static.

Here is the next rule:

Rule 6: Take a few minutes every month to survey current CD rates. Have familiarity with the current yield curve. You will be more knowledgeable when you go to the bank to purchase a CD.

Process suggestion: I consider CDs as semi-cash. I do not want my cash tied up for long periods. I might need that cash for other purposes or to take advantage of an investment opportunity. Accordingly, I only purchase CDs that have a maximum maturity term of one year or less.

My process is to buy a 6-month CD on the first business day of every month. As it is every month, then it means that interest payments, and income, will be every month too. As a CD expires each month, I also increase the amount of the next CD by $1,000. Here is an illustrative summary of a year's activity with all six-month CDs at 4% APR:

CD Amount	Month Purchased	Maturity	Interest Income
$10,000	Jan 2023	July 2023	$200
$10,000	Feb 2023	Aug 2023	$200
$10,000	Mar 2023	Sept 2023	$200
$10,000	April 2023	Oct 2023	$200
$10,000	May 2023	Nov 2023	$200
$10,000	Jun 2023	Dec 2023	$200
$11,000	Jul 2023	Jan 2024	$220
$11,000	Aug 2023	Feb 2024	$220
$11,000	Sept 2023	Mar 2024	$220
$11,000	Oct 2023	April 2024	$220
$11,000	Nov 2023	May 2024	$220
$11,000	Dec 2023	June 2024	$220
$12,000	Jan 2024	July 2024	$240
. . .	. . .	. . .	. . .

Of course, in real life interest rates will vary over that time frame. The chart is to illustrate the process. You can start at any amount, even $1,000, and then follow the pattern. This process accomplishes several things:

- Creates monthly financial awareness and engagement (**Rule 1**).

- Creates a monthly income stream (the overarching goal). If interest rates settle into a narrow range of variability, then the income stream will increase.

- Eliminates tie-up of cash for long periods.

- Puts a process in place, that is repeated over and over. (**Rule 2**).

- Uses a low-risk alternative to create income.

Occasionally I will buy a one-year CD in addition to my normal process. I might have some extra funds available, but I am not sure where to invest them. So, I buy a one-year CD to keep my money working and to have a bonus gift in the future. It depends on the situation. However, I always keep the monthly CD process in place.

Brokered CDs

You can purchase CDs through a broker such as Charles Schwab or Fidelity. These are called *brokered CDs*. The brokerage firm will list perhaps 50 CDs for each maturity term from various banks around the US. Detailed information on each CD, such as the APR, is provided. Brokered CDs are protected by the FDIC as with regular bank CDs.

Brokered CDs are an efficient means to purchase CDs. Sitting at home behind your computer you can survey the listing of many bank CD offerings for each maturity term. APR varies by CD. Within a minute you can purchase the CD that you want. It is very convenient and easy. No online research is necessary. You don't have to go to the bank and complete the forms. You can get the best deal available or make choices between local, regional, and national banks.

Brokered CDs are different in that they can be sold. As interest rates change, a CD could be more or less valuable than the original purchase price. For example, a $10,000 CD at 5% APR will be worth more than $10,000 should prevailing CD APRs fall to 4%. The opposite is also true. A $10,000 CD at 4% will be worth less than $10,000 should the prevailing CD APR rates rise to 5%. The brokerage firm will list the current value of the brokered CD in the account positions listing. This does NOT affect, in any manner, the maturity amount the bank will pay. It only has to do with possibly selling the CD before the maturity date. Brokered CDs provide an interesting alternative should a person want to "cash in" before the maturity date. I encourage the reader to learn more about selling brokered CDs before the maturity date.

Brokered CDs can also be *callable*. It means that the bank can pay off the CD before the maturity date. CDs are designated as callable in the detailed CD specifications. Be sure to read the CD's specifications before purchase to determine whether the CD is callable or not. Banks will offer callable CDs at an APR rate a little higher than the prevailing CD rates. Banks might call a CD when prevailing APR rates have fallen off compared to the CD purchase APR. Banks would not tend to call a CD if rates have risen. I assume banks have internal business rules and algorithms to determine when to call a CD. This is another topic of further learning and research. Until that happens, I suggest buying CDs that are not callable. It is easy to determine from the CD listing details.

Federal and State Taxes

CDs are both federally and state-taxable. They are taxed at ordinary income rates when the payment is made. If you buy a $10,000 5%

one-year maturity CD in January 2024, the bank will pay $10,500 to you in January 2025. Only the return, $500, is taxable for the 2025 tax year.

7

Dividends

Next, I discuss receiving dividends from stocks. This is a great way to create a periodic, sustainable, and reliable income stream. No doubt, creating income from stocks is somewhat riskier than a savings account or CDs. However, the risks can be minimized and the returns can be greater. And that is generally the case: higher risk can mean higher returns.

What exactly is a dividend?

A dividend is a sum of money paid regularly by a company to its shareholders out of its profits or reserve accounts.

A person will receive a dividend payment for every share a person owns of a company that pays a dividend. The more shares that a person owns, the more money they receive. There are two important elements to the definition. The first is that payments are made regularly (if being paid), and second, the payment comes out of profits. If a company is not generally profitable, they will not be paying dividends. Sometimes a company will have a short downturn in profitability, maybe even a loss, and they will still pay a dividend. But that is not a viable long-term situation. The dividend is paid out of cash reserves. Usually, companies pay dividends quarterly during the year. However, some pay monthly or semi-annually.

It is easy to determine if a company pays dividends. Simply go on-line and look at a company's stock profile. Search engines will take you directly to the information. You will find the amount of the dividend and the next payment date. Usually, a company will 'declare' a dividend about 6 weeks in advance of payment. Sometimes it is earlier and sometimes it is later. The 'declaration' means that the company's board of directors has approved the distribution. One more thing: there is a dividend 'X' date. It is the date by which a person has to own the stock to get the next distribution (there is usually a short period between when the stock order is executed and when the stock is owned. Be sure this happens before the 'X' date.) It is part of the 'declaration.'

As a receiver of a dividend, the Income Investor has two options. The dividend can be taken in cash, or it can be reinvested into the stock to buy more shares. The choice is dependent on the current situation. The choice can be changed before the distribution is made. Perhaps there is a need for cash to pay bills or use the cash to invest in another stock. Income Investors often simply reinvest the dividend for years and years, thus building up a significant dividend income stream.

So here is the bottom line: If you buy a stock that distributes regular dividends, you will get a regular quarterly or other, payment from that company. You don't have to do anything more than that.

Here is the next rule.

Rule 7: Create a portfolio of dividend-producing stocks that produce a reliable, consistent, and growing income stream.

That said, there is a lot more to the story. You should learn additional concepts, and how to look for good dividend-producing stock candidates.

Dividend Yield

Dividend yield is the first concept to understand. The dividend yield is the annual dividend paid divided by the current stock price expressed as a percentage. For example, if the dividend payments over the last year have been $4.00 and the current stock price is $100, then the dividend yield is 4%. You can see that dividend yield will change by the minute because stock prices change by the minute. In this case, if the stock price falls to $80, then the dividend yield is 5%. If the stock price goes up to $120, then the dividend yield is 3.33%. The dividend yield is annualized because it includes all the dividends from the past year.

Using the dividend yield allows one to compare two different stocks for attractiveness. Suppose stock 'A' paid $2.00 in dividends over the past year and has a current price of $20, then the dividend yield is 10%. And suppose another stock 'B' paid $5.00 in dividends and has a current price of $90, then the dividend yield is 5.6%. So, it is easy to see stock 'A' is more attractive in terms of income because the dividend yield is higher. This is true even though stock 'B' actually paid more than two times the dividend paid by stock 'A.'

Dividend yield also allows one to compare dividend investing with other alternatives, such as a comparison to a Certificate of Deposit (CD). CD returns are always stated as 'annualized returns.' Suppose a stock has a dividend yield of 3%, and a CD pays 2% annualized interest, then the stock is more attractive. But suppose the CD pays 5% annualized interest, then the CD is more attractive. The same kind of analysis can be applied to other income investment instruments such as bank interest and mutual fund distributions.

As a dividend Income Investor, one should always know the dividend yield for each stock being considered. Also, you should be cognizant of ongoing dividend yields of previously purchased stocks. They are like flashing signals as to the health and well-being of a company. When dividend yields rise dramatically, then it is most likely that the stock price has declined. You should understand why. Usually, it is just normal market fluctuation, and that is okay. If the dividend yield decreases, then it means that the stock price has increased, which is usually a good sign. Again, you should know what is happening and why.

Dividend Growth

Many people are not aware that the best companies increase their dividend distribution each year. The typical annual percentage increase is 3% to 5%. In some cases, it is more than that for a few years as a company experiences revenue growth. Sometimes a company will need to cut their dividend and even suspend a dividend. Dividend growth is an important element in selecting a stock for dividend income.

The most exciting thing for an income investor is when dividend growth is coupled with dividend reinvesting. This leads to a very nice increase in income on a quarterly and yearly basis.

Here is an example showing what can happen even though the stock price never changes. Assume an investor has 100 shares of a $50 stock at the beginning of the analysis period. Therefore, the total investment is $5,000. The stock has a dividend distribution of $2.00 per year for a dividend yield of 4%. At the beginning, a $.50 per share dividend is to be paid every quarter. As the investor has 100 shares it means initially the investor will receive $50.00 each quarter.

If the investor chooses to reinvest dividends, here is what will happen in the first year. Again, for this example, the price of the stock remains constant.

Quarter 1: the investor receives $50, buys more shares at $50, and now has 101 shares.

Quarter 2: the investor receives $50.50, buys more shares at $50, and now has 102.01 shares.

Quarter 3: the investor receives $51.005, buys more shares at $50, and now has 103.03 shares.

Quarter 4: the investor receives $51.52, buys more shares at $50, and now has 104.06 shares.

Now assume the company declares a 4% increase in dividends, which is an increase well within a common range. Therefore, the annual dividend goes from $2.00 to $2.08. The quarterly dividend will now be $.52 per share. Here is what will happen in year 2:

Quarter 1: the investor receives $54.11, buys more shares at $50, and now has 105.14 shares.

Quarter 2: the investor receives $54.67, buys more shares at $50, and now has 106.23 shares.

Quarter 3: the investor receives, $55.24, buys more shares at $50, and now has 107.33 shares.

Quarter 4: the investor receives $55.81, buys more shares at $50, and now has 108.45 shares.

So, in two years, without any intervention by the investor, the dividend has grown by $5.81 or 11.62%. That is great, and it is faster than economic inflation of about 3% per year. And of course, the dividend will likely increase again in the next year, and so on and so on. Notice also that the investor's stock value has increased too. It began at $5,000, and after two years it is $5,422.50. That is because the investor now has more shares. This is without any increase in stock price.

You can see that taking this growth out to ten or 20 years will mean amazing numbers. A single investment of $5,000 will mean a very nice quarterly income down the road. And nothing had to be done other than making the initial investment AND choosing to reinvest dividends. This is the fundamental dividend growth mechanism at work. It is very powerful.

Of course, stock prices do not remain the same. For the example above, the stock was maintained at the same price to illustrate the power of reinvesting and increasing dividend payments. If a stock goes down in price and if the dividend is the same, then more shares will be purchased during reinvestment. At the same time, the overall stock value will decrease too. If a stock increases in price, then fewer shares will be purchased and the overall stock value will increase too. As a company grows revenue and income, then the stock price will likely increase. But just as importantly, the company is more apt to increase the dividend to maintain dividend yield.

State and Federal Taxes

Yes, dividends that are distributed in a regular brokerage account (that is, a non-retirement or non-IRA account) are taxable. They are treated differently from regular income such as wages. There are two types of dividends for tax purposes: qualifying and nonqualifying. 'Qualifying dividends' are subject to special tax considerations, which are usually less than regular income tax rates. 'Nonqualifying dividends' are taxed at the regular tax rates. Exactly what the tax rates are for a given year is dependent on the current tax laws passed by the US Congress. The brokerage account provider should provide a detailed 1099 showing which dividends are qualifying and those that are nonqualifying. Even though dividends are reinvested, as opposed to being taken as cash, they are taxable. If a person is working in a regular job and earning significant dividends, then tax withholding should be adjusted accordingly. Retired people can readily estimate tax payments. Of course, a professional tax accountant can help determine appropriate estimated tax payments. Retired people usually have lower overall income, so the tax implications will be less than for working people.

If cash flow becomes a problem, then the investor can always choose to take the dividend as cash instead of reinvesting. This option can be changed at any time and applies to all following dividend distributions until changed. Sometimes taking the dividend as cash is necessary. There could be many reasons to do this. It could be to pay taxes. That's okay. The thing is, as an investor you have that alternative. Without the dividend income, you do not.

You can shield yourself from current dividend taxes by opening a retirement account, such as a Roth IRA as per Internal Revenue Service rules. Once a deposit is made into a Roth IRA, then individual stocks can be purchased and sold using the brokerage account. Dividends can be reinvested with no tax implications. Be sure to check on current IRS rules for retirement accounts.

Picking Good Dividend Stocks

The next step regarding dividends is to choose good stocks that can deliver repeated income over a long period. This part of the chapter discusses the criteria to do so. You will want to use those criteria to compare stocks with one another. Objective criteria help to remove guessing from the process.

It's important to understand that the criteria being presented are based on fundamental investment concepts and company performance. That is what being an Income Investor is about. This is much different from being an investor who listens to company hype, Internet videos, TV stock pickers, and people who push a stock.

So, here are the important criteria to use when picking a good dividend stock. I consider these primary indicators, and they are the first filter criteria to be used in your analysis.

Pays A Dividend

A stock has to pay a dividend for it to be considered by an Income Investor. It is easy to determine this. There is complete financial information for all publicly traded companies on the Internet. For example, the finance pages of Yahoo.com have complete information. You can have dividend and yield data in seconds.

There are a lot of stocks that do not pay a dividend and probably never will. Those companies keep their cash and reinvest it back into the business for expansion or to service debt. Investors will only make a return if they buy the stock at a price and sell the stock later at a higher price. 'Growth Stock' is a term that has to do with a stock whose price climbs faster than the market indexes. Such stocks do not usually pay a dividend, or if so, very little because they are all about making the company bigger and bigger. Many high-technology stocks and start-ups fall into this category. You cannot expect such stocks to ever pay a dividend. Sometimes, such companies will be bought out by a larger company that does pay a dividend. Usually, the buying company wants intellectual property or specific markets the purchased company has.

Therefore, the first requirement is to find companies that pay dividends.

Earnings

A company pays dividends out of the profits it makes. Therefore, a company has to have a good track record of making money. A publicly traded company will publish earnings every quarter via the income statement. It is easy to look at earnings growth year over year. This data is readily available through the brokerage account data and on public Internet sites. For income investing purposes, a company doesn't need to have incredible earnings growth, but more so, a company should have steady earnings growth.

It is a huge red flag when a company is losing money. A company can continue to pay dividend distributions in the short run, but it is unsustainable. It is best to stay away from companies that are losing money for an initial investment, even though they are currently making dividend distributions. Back away, but continue to monitor the company. Then when things turn around, give them a legitimate consideration.

Dividend Yield Criteria

The dividend yield is the yearly dividend amount divided by the current price of the stock. Dividend yields change by the second because the stock price changes. Dividend yields can vary from 1% to 12%. A solid dividend yield is between 2% to 6%. Higher is not always better. Sometimes a high dividend yield is due to the stock taking a price dive. One should research why that happened. For example, in the spring of 2020, some stock prices fell greatly because of the Covid-19 pandemic shutdown. Consequently, dividend yields went up greatly. If you believed the company would rebound, then it was a great time to invest. You got a great deal. However, some companies never did recover, and they stopped paying dividends altogether.

Other companies pay dividends seemingly forever with an average yield of 3%. They have solid dividend distributions year after year.

Two examples are Johnson and Johnson, the pharmaceutical company, and Exxon Mobil, the energy company. Companies that have a long track record of paying dividends are called "Dividend Aristocrats."

It is very alluring to choose stocks with the highest dividend yields. Real Estate Investment Trusts (REITS) and Business Development Corporations (BDCs) can have dividend yields in the 9-11% range. This sounds great. However, **my suggestion is to invest in such opportunities modestly** and thereby have those investments compose a small part of the overall portfolio. In 2008, the real estate market collapsed. Several REITS went bankrupt. Other companies are exceptionally sensitive to the US economy and therefore might need to cut their dividend significantly. And such companies might not grow their dividend as they have already reached maximum levels. **One strategy is to reduce risk by taking dividends as cash rather than reinvesting.** Consider these stocks as cash generators. Use the cash to invest in other stocks.

Dividend Growth Criteria

As mentioned earlier, some companies will increase their dividend each year. This is because these companies are growing their revenue, income, and cash each year. They pass this success on to their shareholders. We showed earlier how powerful dividend growth can be. Companies that do not grow their dividend are either stagnant or do not care much about their shareholders. They want to reinvest their profits to create growth.

Dividend growth can average between 2% to 12%. As of this writing Lilly Pharmaceuticals has a 3-year dividend growth rate of 12.5% and a 5-year dividend growth rate of 8.2%. That is remarkable. To cite another example, IBM has a 3-year dividend growth rate of 3.3% and a 5-year dividend growth rate of 5.4%. Dividend growth rates are typically in the 3-5% range.

Your brokerage account should provide you with this data. Sustained dividend growth is a very good indicator of a stock to buy for an Income Investor.

Price Earnings Ratio (PER or PE)

PER is the price of the stock divided by the earnings per share of the stock. It is also called 'the multiple,' or restated, price as a multiple of earnings. Low PER values are great and high PERs make an investor take pause. Low PERs mean that the price of the stock is low compared to the earnings per share. It says that the stock is 'undervalued.' Conversely, a high PER means that the price is high compared to earnings. The stock is considered 'overvalued.' Growth stocks often have high PER values because they are undergoing expansion and the market believes it will continue.

Low PERs are typically under 20. High PERs are 40-50 and up. Then there is the midrange between 20 to 40, where an investor might say that the stock is 'fairly valued.' PERs tend to vary by industry. High-tech companies, which have a lot of growth, usually have high PER values. For example, Tesla (TSLA) has a current PER of 46.5. Utility companies, which have slow growth, have low PER values. For example, American Electric Power (AEP) has a current PER of 18.7.

I favor companies with lower PERs because usually the stock price will remain the same or go up. It is 'under-valued.' While I like to focus on income, it is also important to protect the underlying value of the stock. It makes little sense to get a big dividend from a stock that could fall greatly in value. **High PER stocks are very susceptible to bad news.** Quite often, such stocks have high PERs because of market excitement. If any bad news comes about, exuberance will disappear and the stock will fall like a stone.

52-Week High

Related to PER is the relation of the current stock price to the 52-week high historical price. There is a correlation between PER and this relationship. When a stock is at or near its 52-week high price, then the PER is going to be as high as it is going to go in the near term. That makes me uncomfortable because stock prices cannot stay at their 52-week high price forever.

I like stocks that are off their 52-week high 10-20% as long as there are nonthreatening reasons for it. That is, no seismic events are happening. Many times, it is just normal stock market cycles. A stock is 'out of favor' for some reason. Investment companies take money out of one area and put it in another repeatedly. Or maybe there was some bad news, which could be temporary. For example, a pharmaceutical company might get some negative news on a new drug they are developing. The stock market will sell off the stock to some extent. However, maybe the company just has to do more research, and then the company will rebound nicely. I view these cases as potential buying opportunities because I see value in the purchase. The downside risk of the stock is reduced somewhat.

It is important to understand why a stock fell off from its high value. It might take a little research, but it is worth it. You could make a great investment and thereby increase your return. It's called 'buying on the dips.' Many years ago, Caterpillar popped up on my stock screener because the yield was around 5%. The price of the stock had fallen dramatically to around $30 per share. I did some research and concluded that Caterpillar, being an excellent company, would overcome their temporary issues and rebound. I started to buy shares and continued to do so as it rose in price. I stopped buying shares when the yield went below 4%, which was around a stock price of $50. The current price of Caterpillar is $281. Caterpillar continues to pay a dividend to me every quarter.

When stock prices are off their 52-week high, then the dividend yield will be higher too. Investment in the company at that point will result in years of returns.

Secondary Measures and Considerations

Beyond the primary indicators, there are some additional pieces of information to consider. They might raise a red flag or be a tie-breaker between two or three candidate stocks. Companies could look great using the primary indicators, but there could be problems lurking that affect future returns. Here are three additional factors to consider.

Debt to Equity Ratio (DER)

This ratio is an indicator of how much a given company is using debt to finance operations rather than using normal business flow. Long-term debt is especially an issue because it will have a drag on profits for years in the future. Debt must be serviced in some manner. It is not an option. Debt payment must either be paid in the near term or refinanced for the long term.

Debt levels vary by industry. Some industries can support high levels of debt because they have consistent and sustainable revenue streams. An example of a high debt-level industry is utilities. They have to support massive infrastructures, and yet they have a solid revenue stream. They can use debt to expand as necessary. Other companies can support high debt levels in the short term, but could have major problems should there be a downturn in the economy. Should their revenue stream be diminished, they would not be able to make debt payments.

It is best to compare DER levels between companies within the same industry. Recently I found a pharmaceutical company with excellent primary dividend indicators. It looked great, but I found that its DER ratio was significantly higher than other pharmaceutical companies. I didn't feel comfortable buying the stock because I was concerned it could not sustain the dividend for the long term. I was concerned they were using debt as a major element to achieving success. I did not buy the stock.

I encourage and advise readers to spend a little time understanding DER. There are many online references and are easy to understand.

The DER is easily calculated using balance sheet data, which is readily available. Analyst reports usually have DER values calculated as part of the provided metrics. Analyst reports also discuss how much debt there is and what the company is doing to service it.

Process suggestion: Get acquainted with normal range DER values for an industry in which you want to purchase shares. Get a feel for outlier values. Perhaps keep values on a spreadsheet as you do research. Then they will be easily available in the future. DER values are not going to change quickly, and you are likely to find that most companies within an industry will have DER close to the average. (Or more precisely, within one standard deviation of the mean.) Therefore, outliers can be spotted quickly.

Forward PER

The forward price earnings ratio (FPER) incorporates analyst's estimates of earnings per share in the next quarter or year. It is generally calculated by dividing the current stock price by the sum of the previous three earnings per share quarters plus the next forecasted earnings per share. FPER is usually readily available in online stock data. So, you won't have to do the calculation.

If a company has forecasted increasing earnings per share, then the FPER will be lower than the current PER. As mentioned previously, earnings are key to dividend distributions. Increasing earnings will likely mean increasing dividend payouts, which is exactly what you want. **However, if FPER is higher than the current PER, then this is a red flag.** Further research is required. Read the analyst reports to understand why the forecast is for decreasing earnings. Perhaps this is a temporary condition, or perhaps it is a sign of long-term issues.

FPER is a good tiebreaker between two prospective stock purchases for dividend income purposes. The stock with the lower FPER is probably the better value buy. I also like stocks with low PER and

FPER values (less than 20), because it means the stock is priced at a good value. Consequently, the stock price is not likely to erode very much, thereby protecting the worth of the stock in your portfolio.

Price to Book Ratio

The price-to-book ratio (PBR) compares the price of the stock to the book value per share. It is a mixture of the market price of the stock and balance sheet values. It is usually available as a calculated value by online services. You will need to look for it.

PBR is used by value investors to identify opportunities. If the price of the stock is low compared to a company's assets, then the company appears to be a good buy. PBR is very much industry-related. Accounting rules, capital requirements, and market sentiment vary greatly from one industry to another. As discussed previously, it is a good idea to focus and learn about specific industries for investment purposes. You will learn what are good PBR numbers for an industry.

As with other ratios, PBR serves as a tiebreaker between two stock purchase candidates within an industry. I encourage you to spend a little time researching PBR to gain more knowledge. Analysts consider PBR significantly, so it is a good idea to understand their thinking.

Analyst Recommendations

Finally, it is time to consider additional comments and recommendations from other experts. It has been amazing how many times I reached this point with two or three stock candidates and found 'Buy' or 'Strong Buy' recommendations. The important point is that you will be coming from an Income Investor point of view. You have done your screening for that purpose. Now you seek a different perspective and confirmation. Note this is quite different from initially scanning for 'Buy' recommendations on the Internet and then buying a stock based solely on one report. As an Income Investor, you have income on your mind. You have done your work to get to this point.

After you have narrowed your choices to a small number of stock buy candidates, then the last step is to read the analyst reports. Each analyst company has a different rating scale. Analyst reports will summarize current activities and support their rating. It will give you insights such as new drugs in a pipeline, investments, buyouts, mergers, stock buybacks, and other corporate actions. Analyst reports usually have a price target, which you can compare to the current price. It might very well be that the target price has already been reached. The date of the analyst report is very important. Much could have changed if the analyst report is a few months old. You want to be sensitive to the date of the analyst report.

I use analyst reports as a tie-breaker between investment candidates, and to identify any red flags I missed. They make me feel more confident in my choice.

Rule 8: Read at least one analyst report before purchasing a stock.

Screening Processes

It is critically important to have an efficient stock screening process in place to create an energized income-producing stream. The idea is to apply the criteria mentioned previously to hundreds of stocks, which will produce a small list of candidate stocks for purchase. Out of that list, the top two or three stocks will be picked for further research. The tie-breaker criteria and analyst reports will help to determine the final choice.

Rule 9: Have a stock screener method in place so that a large number of stocks can be easily and quickly evaluated using selection criteria. Refine the criteria over time.

The goal of using a stock screener is to quickly and objectively consider a large number of stocks that match the filter criteria. Remember:

Rule 2: Adopt solid investment processes, and use them over and over.

An efficient and easy-to-use stock screener will mean you are more likely to be engaged, which gets back to **Rule 1**. Once your stock screener is active and configured, then within an hour you should be able to find suitable stock candidates for purchase. That time estimate includes reviewing analyst reports for the top two or three best stocks. I suggest you include ALL of the primary criteria listed above for initial screening: earnings, pays a dividend, dividend yield, dividend growth, PER, and off 52-week high. **Using dividend yield alone, while highly enticing, is not a good idea.** Review previous comments to understand why.

Stock Screener Alternatives

Free Online Stock Screeners. It is easy to search for and find free online dividend stock screeners. I have not evaluated many of them. I did find that many of them have limited criteria that can be entered. There is not a lot of flexibility. And of course, there is usually the selling proposition involved. You will likely have to provide contact information such as an email address to use the screener.

Brokerage Company Stock Screeners. I use the Charles Schwab stock screener, which is robust with the filtering criteria it offers. I can store named filtering criteria screeners. With just a click of the mouse, the stock screener is activated and results are produced. I can then sort the list by criteria so I can examine the list from different perspectives. I know that other brokerage companies have similar stock screener tools.

DIY Stock Screener. A couple of years ago, I wrote a software program that gathers stock data using a web service and then performs analysis on the data. The results are written into a spreadsheet. The benefit of this approach is that I was able to do a more detailed and insightful analysis. For example, I was able to calculate industry averages for the debt-to-equity ratio (DER, see previous comments), and then determine company outliers using standard deviation. I was also able to weigh the various selection criteria and develop an overall rating score. This is an alternative for those who can write code and have knowledge of accessing and consuming web services. Web service companies usually have an active developer community and example code to help the process along. The first time I ran my program I made enough money to pay for the web service fees many times over.

Industry Focus

As I mentioned previously, I strongly recommend that new Income Investors start by focusing on an industry. That way, you will become knowledgeable of industry leaders and understand their market environment. You can make better-informed comparisons between stock purchase candidates. I guarantee you that there will be several opportunities within an industry for your consideration. Restricting efforts to a specific industry is not a limitation on possible income streams. Here are three industries to consider as a starting point: utilities, pharmaceuticals, and financial institutions. Any of those industries will keep you busy for quite a while.

Rule 10. Focus on specific industries rather than a shotgun approach across the entire stock market.

Hopefully, your stock screener will allow you to use 'Industry' as a means of selecting stocks.

Process suggestion: Choose an industry, and create a spreadsheet list of all of the companies within that industry. It will take less than an hour using an Internet search. For example, search on "pharmaceutical stocks that pay dividends." Tons of search results will be returned. As you gather more data about companies then add that data to the spreadsheet. This is not your stock screener, but more so, an ongoing data and notes collection area. It is a way to get started.

Data gathering can take place over months and years as you continue to edit the spreadsheet. Just this one step will be highly educational and informative. You will know all the game players and leaders within an industry. You will make conclusions, intuitively and logically. You will be engaged in creating income. Yes, it will be a little time-consuming, but let us remember **Rule 1** again. And it is easy. All you are doing is recording information in a spreadsheet for future and easy reference.

Tracking and Goals

Tracking progress and setting goals are the two most important process steps. Here are the next two rules:

Rule 11. Track every dividend payment in a spreadsheet.

Rule 12. Set dividend income goals at the beginning of the year. Periodically compare goal objectives to actual results.

It isn't enough to simply look at brokerage statements. It is best to make dividend payment entries in a spreadsheet. By doing so, you will know:

- The expected dividend declaration and payment dates.

- What quarter dividend increases are usually declared.

- The amount of dividend increase.

- If a company is missing or not increasing dividends.

- Estimated dividend amounts for the remainder of the year.

This information will make you a more active and knowledgeable investor. You will be actively engaged and quicker to pick up on developments that could affect income. For example, if you can project income for the remainder of the year, then you can make the necessary moves to meet goals. Making an entry in a spreadsheet takes a few minutes, but it makes a huge difference in results.

Below is an example of a dividend tracking spreadsheet as of January 30, 2024.

	A	B	C	D	E	F	G
2	Company	Dates	First Quarter 2024	Second Quarter 2024	Third Quarter 2024	Fourth Quarter 2024	Total Year
4	StockA-1	Jan,Ap,Jul,O-8th	20.00	22.70	22.70	22.70	88.10
5	StockA-2	Jan,Ap,Jul,O-13th	55.60	57.13	57.13	57.13	226.99
6	StockA-3	Jan,Ap,Jul,O-20th	167.50	168.47	168.47	168.47	672.91
7	StockB-1	F,May,Au,N-1st	76.38	76.38	76.38	76.38	305.52
8	StockB-2	F,May,Au,N-2nd	643.64	643.64	643.64	643.64	2574.56
9	StockB-3	F,May,Au,N-10th	27.02	27.02	27.02	27.02	108.08
10	StockC-1	Mar,Jun,S,D-5th	23.41	23.41	23.41	23.41	93.64
11	StockC-2	Mar,Jun,S,D-6th	7.07	7.07	7.07	7.07	28.28
12	StockC-3	Mar,Jun,S,D-7th	16.28	16.28	16.28	16.28	65.12
13							
14	StockA-1 Special Dividend	1/8/2024	1.50				
15							
16							
17	Total Stocks		1038.40	1042.10	1042.10	1042.10	4163.20
18	Goal		950.00	1075.00	1200.00	1350.00	4575.00
19	Goal Variance		88.40	-32.90	-157.90	-307.90	-411.80
20							
21							

The columns of the spreadsheet are:

- Name of company and/or stock symbol.

- Month and Date sequence. Companies will pay a dividend in the first, second, or third month of the quarter. The number is the approximate date when the payment is made. This can vary plus or minus five days depending on business calendars.

- First, Second, Third, and Fourth Quarter actual and estimated dividend payment amounts. For example, when an actual payment is made in the first quarter the remaining three quarter's payments can be estimated.

- Total. The total amount of the four quarter payments. It includes both actual and estimated payments. It will change as the actual and estimated payments change during the year.

Going down the spreadsheet, you see that the companies are arranged in order of payment calendar. The stocks in the upper rows are the first month of the quarter payment companies. Stocks in the lower rows make payments near the end of the quarter. There is space for 'special dividends,' which companies pay when they have windfall profits. I don't consider them as part of ongoing dividend projections or planning. They are gifts to you as a shareholder but do not expect them every year.

The 'Total Stocks' row is the total dividend payments for the quarter.

Reinvested dividend projections. When a company's dividend is reinvested, then the following quarter's dividend projections are calculated by multiplying the new total number of shares by the current dividend distribution per share. You can see the ripple effect of reinvesting dividends in the first quarter as the dividend payment projections are increased in the second, third, and fourth quarters. In this example, StockA-1, StockA-2, and StockA-3 had dividend payments in January, which were reinvested. Accordingly, the estimated dividend payments for the second, third, and fourth quarters are higher than the first quarter. The remainder of the stocks have not yet had a dividend distribution in 2024. Therefore, the second, third, and fourth quarter dividend payments are unchanged.

Two additional things I do:

- Color code the spreadsheet cells: plain tan is the general downstream projection, yellow means the dividend declaration amount, blue is the dividend reinvested amount, and no color is an actual payment. A cell will go through a standard color progress: tan -> yellow -> no color, or blue -> yellow -> no color. As this book is in black and white, the colors are not seen. You can choose a color scheme that works for you.

- Border: a cell with a border is the quarter in which a previous increase in dividend occurred. This helps greatly when to look for dividend increases. Usually, this needs to be done one time as most companies are very regular and timely concerning dividend payments. For example, StockC-1 is expected to have an increased dividend in the second quarter. However, the new dividend amount has not been declared yet.

Again, the reason for this process is to keep aware and engaged in the income generation process. It seems like a lot of work. However, tracking takes just a few minutes per month. And it is exciting and fun to see income increase month after month. Again, it is a PROCESS.

Goals

Setting goals is the next part of the process. Setting goals that cannot be made is a waste of time. It will just lead to frustration. Setting goals that are too low is not aggressive enough. There is a middle ground in which solid income development progress can be made. You want some 'stretching' so that you have to work a little to meet them.

Dividend income goals for all quarters should be set at the beginning of the year. Progress toward achieving goals should be reviewed monthly. The objective is to exceed income goals each quarter and thereby exceed goals for the year. (See Appendix C.)

Goals should be specified at the bottom of the spreadsheet. It should calculate the variance from the goals so you know where you stand at all times. As the year moves along you will make investment adjustments as necessary.

Look at the spreadsheet focusing on the bottom rows. You will see that the Income Investor has set goals for each quarter starting at $950 in the first quarter and increasing to $1,350 in the last quarter. This investor has a dividend payment goal of $4,575 for the year.

The first quarter dividend payment projection is $1038.40, which means the goal for the first quarter is exceeded by $88.40. The second quarter goal has not yet been met as the current projection is less than the goal by $32.90. However, as the date of the spreadsheet is January 30th, the income investor can make additional investments to reach the second quarter goal, which ends on June 30th. And no doubt, the six dividend payments yet to be made in the first quarter will be reinvested and therefore help to reach the goal in the second quarter. All of those six stocks will have increased payouts in the second quarter.

You see that the third and fourth quarters are further below their respective goals. The Income Investor should make the necessary investments during the year to reach those goals. This is exactly what Income Investors should do: set goals and then work at meeting them. It is a constant and recurring process. It is **Rule 2** in action.

Process Suggestion: I look at my dividend tracking spreadsheet periodically throughout the month. I research new stocks using my stock screener. I consider where I am concerning the quarterly goals. I develop a little plan. On the first business day of the month, I make new dividend income-related investments. This is how I **"give myself a raise every month."** And it is the subtitle of this book. Even if it is just a few additional shares of a stock I already own, I am always increasing my income. When I have made my investments, I enter the dividend payment estimates into the spreadsheet and reflect on where I am concerning the goals. I then start the process of getting ready for the next month.

For some of you, this process will seem as though it is too much effort. However, once you get it in place, it will seem easy and fun. You will gain a sense of the market and know what stocks are worth evaluating. You can run your stock screener a couple of times during the month and see if there are any rising stars. Always remember, **Rule 1: If you are not concerned about your money, don't expect anyone else to be.** All told it will probably consume 1-2 hours of your time each month, which is very modest compared to the great returns you will reap. Purchasing the stock and entering the data into the spreadsheet will take about 15 minutes. The remainder of the time will be looking for and thinking about your next opportunity. When the first business day of the month comes you will be jumping at the bit to make your investments and go after your goals.

Do I only do dividend investing trades on the first business day of the month? The answer is yes. I do this because I want to adhere to my process. It's a mindset. It is **Rule 2: Adopt solid investment processes, and use them over and over.** I don't want to vary from something that works. The schedule is part of the process.

Do I make stock purchases only on the first business day of the month? The answer is no. Occasionally there are special situations and opportunities such that I have to take advantage of them. I consider these purchases as wealth-building opportunities as opposed to income-building. For example, in the spring of 2020, many stocks tanked because of the Covid-19 pandemic. The economy was in freefall as people sold their stocks. I saw this as an opportunity to buy former high-priced stocks cheaply. (Dividend yields were of secondary importance.) My view was that the pandemic would come and go, and then the stocks would rebound. As the stock prices moved downward, I continued to invest thereby reducing the average cost of my investment for that stock. I was correct. In 2024 the pandemic is history and the stock prices have rebounded, and then some. The point is that while you have a process that you follow without fail, always be looking for special opportunities of which you can take advantage.

8

Collective Funds

Collective Funds are collections of stocks or investment instruments that are managed and sold by a third party. Mutual funds, Exchange Traded Funds (ETFs), Standard and Poor's Depository Receipts (SPDRs), and index funds fall into this category.

These vehicles usually focus on a specific area of the stock market or a particular kind of investment. For example, there are S&P index funds that try to follow the general growth track of the stock market, which has generally been upward over the last 100 years. A person who buys such funds expects to have similar wealth percentage gains over the long term. Other funds might be composed of high-tech or growth stocks. In this case, the investor would want to participate in emerging new technologies. In general, investment houses will develop products that are attractive to investors by combining stocks in various ways under a theme. Then they are marketed as such.

Collective funds provide a valuable wealth improvement alternative, especially for the casual investor. They do the following:

- Reduce risk because the fund is a *collection* of stocks. It is not dependent on the performance of any one of them. Risk is spread out among the stocks in the fund.

- Uses the management expertise of investment professionals who have insight and understanding of their fund's focus.

- Provide a product that identifies with an investor's area of interest. For example, a young investor might want to participate in high-tech growth opportunities without needing to research specific companies.

However, from an Income Investor point of view, collective funds are not a good match. There are important reasons for this:

- Because the fund is managed by a third party, fees will be extracted to pay for that service. Employees are highly paid for their work which requires expertise and long hours of effort. Fund performance is paramount. However, management fees will reduce fund payments to the investor.

- Actual payment distributions (or dividends) cannot be forecasted. It is up to the fund managers to determine what they will be. Therefore, it is difficult for the Income Investor to establish goals and reliably invest to make them. I have a fund that paid thousands of dollars one year, and then the next two years it paid zero. Collection funds are NOT typically a reliable and consistent income stream of the kind the Income Investor wants.

- Because the fund is a collection of stocks or instruments, returns will be affected by the winners AND losers. More stocks in the fund's portfolio will mean less risk, but it will also mean more average returns. You have to take the good with the bad.

- You have no control over the composition of the portfolio. Therefore, the investor is dependent on a third party for results. It is somewhat a violation of **Rule 1**. You are placing your faith in fund management to provide returns.

I invest in a few collective funds that provide means to participate in specific areas, especially those that are difficult mechanically to execute. For example, I invest in a municipal bond fund. Fund managers buy municipal bonds from all over the country (and US territories), and package them into a single investment opportunity.

Buying individual municipal bonds is beyond my current effort scope and time.

The municipal bond fund pays a monthly distribution, which I reinvest. It pays a 4-6% yield depending on the month. Both the price of the fund's share and the distribution per share can vary each month. Consequently, the yield can have significant swings.

The attractive quality of this fund is that the income is not federally taxable. Being a fund, it lowers the risk of a local municipality defaulting on bond payments and interest. Therefore, I can participate in community and regional growth easily with low risk. Of course, as usual with a collective fund, the fund management has significantly increased and decreased the monthly distribution subject to their algorithms and decisions. It has happened several times with little or no notice. Therefore, only general distribution forecasts can be made. Consequently, it is not part of what I consider my income-producing strategy and is a very tiny piece of my portfolio. I get what income I can get. I am not going to be dependent on it.

My recommendation regarding collection funds is to consider them as wealth-building alternatives rather than income-producing options. Consider the focus of the fund and its long-term growth potential and wealth return. They are not good for reliably predicting the next quarter's actual distribution because fund management can adjust it with little or no notification. If you get a distribution, then reinvest it and build wealth.

This leads to the next rule:

Rule 13: Do not make collective funds part of the income-producing process. Use them for long-term wealth building.

Part III — Next Steps

9

How to Get Started

Here is a game plan to get you started to become an Income Investor.

Step 1

Start by remembering **the overarching goal is to develop a sustainable, consistent, and predictable income stream.** It is the kind of income that can be used to make a car payment, pay utility bills, or put food on the table. It is money that can be counted on to improve one's life. It is money that can be used to make retirement better.

The Income Investor makes it happen by researching, tracking, goal setting, and making intelligent investments. The Income Investor uses a repeating and efficient process to achieve success. It is based on a logical analysis of fundamental monetary and corporate metrics such as interest rates, earnings, yield, and stock value.

The Income Investor clearly understands the distinction between wealth-building and income-growing. Wealth-building focuses on increasing the overall worth of one's assets. It includes the value of properties, money in the bank, and stock and bond holdings. Income growth relates to **new money** coming in the door every month. The Income Investor focuses on the latter and does not get off track or confused about the overarching goal.

Rule 14: Understand the difference between wealth-building and income-growing.

So, step one is to have the Income Investor mindset. You want to get completely focused on what you want to achieve.

Step 2

The second step is to acquire the three essential tools: a calculator, a spreadsheet program, and a brokerage account. They were discussed earlier. Know how to use the spreadsheet program. Review various brokerage companies using the features discussed earlier, and then open an account with the required financial deposit. Get acquainted with the interface. Learn how to execute basic operations such as researching stock statistics, reading analyst reports, buying stocks, or moving money.

Step 3

Get a stock screening process in place. This is probably the most difficult step. You want to be able to enter filter criteria, such as yield and PER, and the program will produce a list of stocks meeting that requirement. As I mentioned previously, Charles Schwab has a stock screener which supports numerous filter elements. It also supports named saved stock screeners, such as "My Power Company Screener." Once the screener has been configured, a new list of stock investment candidates can be found within a second. Fidelity also has a stock screener with very detailed filter elements that can be custom-selected. It also has prepackaged 'themes,' the user can select. It seems to be a robust tool. I suspect that most major brokerage firms have stock screeners as a standard feature. I also mentioned earlier in the book that there are free online stock screeners that may deserve further scrutiny.

This is a critical step toward being a successful Income Investor. You need to be efficient so that you execute your process easily and repeatedly. Once your stock screener is operational, you will be excited to run it often to see what new candidate investment opportunities pop up.

Step 4

Now that you have the operational tools in place, the next step is to invoke **Rule 2**:

Rule 2: Adopt solid investment processes, and use them over and over.

The three elements of your process are:

- *Process Steps.* You want to plan the specific activities you will do every time. Please refer to the 'Process Suggestions' throughout the book for ideas. If you repeat the process steps each time, then you will do them faster and faster.

- *Process Frequency.* Determine how often you want to run your process and then make a commitment to do it without fail. Perhaps put reminder notifications on your calendar. My thought is to **"give myself a raise every month."** That sparks me to keep going. And once you start to see positive results you will be energized to start the next cycle. Executing the process regularly is very important to ultimate success.

- *Regular Fund Support.* Make provisions to have regular funds available to take advantage of the next income-producing investment opportunity. Even if the funds are modest at the beginning, that is okay. **The process is important.** You will be started. As I mentioned, decades ago I had my paycheck directly deposited into my Charles Schwab account. It changed my perspective of investing from being a secondary activity to a primary activity. Funds are always available, so I used them. No doubt, this would be uncomfortable for a lot of people. Therefore, make an effort to regularly deposit funds into the brokerage account to support the process. And if you are buying CDs, then do so on a regular schedule.

Step 5

Execute your process, invest, and initiate tracking and goal setting using a spreadsheet. **Start by investing slowly and modestly.** Follow your investment. Get a feel for market dynamics. If the stock price goes down, do not panic. If you follow solid practices as previously outlined and it is a good stock as it should be, then it will be fine. It is income that is most important. You are building an income stream. And remember that if the stock price goes down somewhat, the dividend/reinvestment process will buy more of the stock at a lower price. This averages down your investment. Good companies almost always rebound from adversity. They have really smart people working for them.

Step 6

After a year, you are off and running. You are rounding out your portfolio and increasing your goals year over year. You are branching out from one industry to several industries. The growth in dividends is achieving an increased income stream every quarter. Just keep doing it, over and over. Maintain the process.

10

Handling Adversity

Over the last four years, events occurred which adversely affected financial markets and stocks. There was a worldwide pandemic. There have been huge swings in oil prices and rampant inflation. The stock market took a dive and then recovered.

Sometimes, specific industries or individual stocks are affected. Government regulations can change thereby affecting an industry. A good example is when the US Government deregulated the airline industry in the late 1970s. All airlines and airplane manufacturers were affected. As another example, banking regulations can change which have important impacts on individual banks depending on how they are financially structured. Most companies are regulated in some fashion, and the point is that those regulations can change.

Individual companies usually go through cycles. Their revenues can increase, level off, and even decrease. They can have debt issues. Perhaps the costs of raw materials and resources change. While many companies weather such cycles as a normal course of business, some need to take drastic action such as restructuring, selling off assets, layoffs, and management changes. Their dividend payments could be significantly reduced or even eliminated.

There is no doubt that there will be future events that could have an impact on your income-producing goals. Rather than being frustrated and angry with your bad luck, it is better to think and plan. If a specific company in your portfolio has financial issues, then you might take specific action. It depends on the situation.

There are actions to take before and after adversity strikes. First, I talk about minimizing the effects of challenging events by taking preemptive actions *before* something bad happens.

Blending

You will want to have a mixture of fixed, low-risk income generators (such as CDs) and somewhat higher-risk dividend-producing stocks. That is, you will want to *blend* them. The blending percentages are a matter of one's tolerance for risk. Fixed-income securities will usually have a lower yield or return than what is achievable with stocks. If the fixed income portion of your portfolio is too high, then you will be missing out on income opportunities in the present and the future. If the dividend stock portion is very high, then the income stream could be threatened by severe economic downturns. Maybe some stocks will have to suspend dividends. This is exactly what happened with Disney during the COVID-19 pandemic. Here is a new rule to follow:

Rule 15: Blend income production between fixed-income securities and dividend-producing stocks.

Diversity

As I have mentioned, initially focus on an industry. Implement the process suggestions. However, over time you will want to branch out into additional industries. I started with pharmaceuticals. About forty years ago I was reading a book that said that "pharmaceutical companies have the best return on sales of all companies." That sounded pretty good to me! I never forgot that passage. I began accumulating pharmaceutical company stocks, and they became the backbone of my portfolio. Since then, I have branched out to energy/power companies and financial institutions with several stocks in each industry.

Let us remember that macroeconomic developments, government policies, and regulations can often affect all companies within an industry. So, you want to adopt this rule –

Rule 16: Branch out to additional industries over time.

Even with your hard work, research, and adherence to the process, some stocks within your portfolio will have an issue or challenging time. In the pharma industry, it could be additional competition for a specific drug that hurts the revenue stream and profits. In the power industry, there might be wildfires that devastate electrical infrastructure. In the airline industry, maybe the FAA deems a specific airplane as unsafe and grounds it. The obvious answer to mitigate the effect of such events is to diversify within an industry.

You want to work toward having at least three to five stocks within an industry in your portfolio. Of course, you are going to observe the best practices for purchase as outlined previously. So, it might take some time to achieve that kind of diversity. Stocks will ebb and flow over time. The price will change. The PER will change. The yield will change. With patience, you will find good opportunities to initiate investment. This is one of the great benefits of being industry-aware and having efficient stock screening processes. Suddenly, a great opportunity will jump out of nowhere and you can strike to take advantage.

Rule 17: Diversify your industry stock portfolio. And always follow best purchase practices.

Now consider what to do *after* adversity strikes. You have several options.

Specific Stock Actions

The Income Investor needs to monitor the dividend-producing stocks in the portfolio. A great time to do this is when the quarterly payments are made. A quick scan of analyst reports, news, and projections is appropriate. Given that stocks were originally selected with a positive dividend growth rate, there are action levels as follows:

Case 1: Situation normal

- Dividends are being declared and paid.

- Dividends are on track to increase once per year.

- Earnings are growing.

*Additional consideration*s: If the yield is good, the PER is low, and the stock price is off 52-week highs, then consider buying additional stock. Perhaps you can take advantage of a normal cyclical and short-term dip to average down your investment per share.

Case 2: No Dividend Increase

- Dividends are being declared and paid.

- Dividends are not increased for more than four quarters.

- Earnings are stagnant, or slightly decreasing.

Actions: This is the first danger signal. Sometimes companies will run into cash shortages or they want to spend cash on things other than paying dividends. Examples are: spending cash on capital equipment to be more competitive, reducing debt, or buying back stock. As the company is paying the existing dividend, it usually doesn't mean the Income Investor needs to take drastic action. It's a good idea to read analyst reports to gather more information. There is a chance that dividends will again grow in the future. Usually, it is best in the near term to continue to monitor the stock.

Case 3: Dividends Are Reduced or Suspended

- Dividends may be declared but reduced from former amounts

- Earnings are reduced

- A significant event has occurred, which impacts corporate stability.

- Stock price has dropped, and therefore underlying asset value has decreased.

Actions: These events should trigger high interest in the Income Investor. You need to understand what happened. There are probably many news articles available to provide details. Usually, this action by a company comes as a surprise to the general public. There is little if any, prior notice.

Your subsequent actions are to either sell the stock or continue to own the stock. **It depends on the situation.** In 2022, Disney suspended their dividend because the Covid-19 pandemic prevented people from visiting its theme parks. I decided NOT to sell the stock because I felt this had nothing to do with Disney's management or general financial trends. I felt that after the Covid-19 pandemic ended Disney would rebound. In 2024, they reinstituted the dividend. Their latest earnings report is positive.

However, General Electric is a different story. In 2008, GE was having problems. The stock was falling in price and the dividend was cut significantly. My GE stock value fell into a loss status. I did some reading and concluded that I didn't like the direction the company was taking. It was not the same company of which I initially purchased the stock. I decided to sell all of my stock, and then reinvest the funds into another stock. I took a loss, but the loss was a long-term loss, which reduced my income taxes. I remember liking my decision several months after making it. It was a good move.

This is another rule:

Rule 18: Monitor stocks quarterly when the dividend is paid. Be sensitive to changes in the dividend payment amount. Take appropriate action.

In summary, take preemptive action to reduce risk to your income stream. If adversity strikes, take appropriate action to the situation.

11

Finally

The concepts I have presented in this book are not theories. They are actions that I have done for the last 35 years. They are processes that I have executed "over and over." I went from a scattershot investor following the hyped advice of TV "pundits" to an organized and process-oriented investor. I do my research and follow my logic. It's based on the most fundamental economic principles of looking for companies that make earnings and have value. The result is that I have created a solid and growing income stream. My overarching goal is to **"give myself a raise every month."**

I did not write this book to make money. I wrote this book to share what has worked and continues to work for me in practice. I have priced it modestly. I want to spread the knowledge. I hope people who read this book get a different perspective on investing and adopt solid processes to make a steady income. Those of you in the younger age range will benefit hugely because you have decades for your investment incomes to grow. Those of you in the more elderly age range will benefit because you can add income to your pension and Social Security payments. In all cases, a solid and growing income stream makes life better.

Good investing to everyone. **"Give yourself a raise every month."**

Appendix A

Industry Focus: Energy Utilities

Companies within the same industry generally face the same regulatory rules and the same market forces. Therefore, within a general range, their dividend distribution profiles will be similar. Yes, some companies have better performance than others and they will have different stock prices and metrics. It is for the investor to do current research and analysis to make an educated and informed investment. It is a good idea to focus on an industry so that you can make more informed investments. Here, I look at the 'Energy Utility' sector. What I discuss is the kind of thinking people should apply to any industry. Learn the following things about an industry:

- What companies are the leaders and why?

- What are the industry growth opportunities?

- What are the macroeconomic trends affecting the industry?

- What regulations affect the industry?

- Is the industry focused only in the US or is it worldwide?

- What are typical financial metrics for industry companies?

Reading company analyst reports will provide most of this information because these factors have a direct bearing on future income.

Analysts will incorporate this information to constitute 'sell, hold, or buy' signals. Within a very short time, an income investor can gain an informed and broad understanding of how an industry operates.

Utilities are companies that provide general services to the community such as power, water, and gas. They have a monopoly that covers a specific territory because it is not reasonable to achieve competition by duplicating electric, water, and gas lines. Therefore, utilities are regulated by locally governed public service commissions. Utilities are allowed to achieve a regulated profit, that is a return, based on their invested capital, which is all of their massive infrastructure. Public service commissions set service rates appropriately to achieve that return.

In particular, electric utilities have lots of invested capital such as transmission lines, power plants, dams, substations, windmills, and solar farms. Electric service rates paid by users provide revenue to cover costs, depreciation, and overhead. The profit made, if any, should match the regulated return that is allowed. Dividends are paid out of the profits to the utility's stockholders.

To a lot of investors, power utilities are not very exciting. However, they are solid performers because they have a monopoly and people always need and will pay for electric power. Furthermore, electric power needs are going to increase because there is sentiment toward electrically powered vehicles and a growing economy requires growing energy resources. These are macro trends. Therefore, we can expect increased electric utility expenditures to provide the needed production capacity. It is also reasonable to expect that electricity rates will also increase.

Here are some general numbers:

- Dividend yield: 2-6%

- PER: 10-25 (remember, lower is better).

- Dividend growth: 2-5%

- Slow increase in stock price

Power utilities are a good starting point for income investing. Risks are low and returns are solid. Many utilities have long track records of paying AND growing their dividend. The main part of this book shows how reinvesting and dividend growth can provide a powerful return in a short time even if the stock price doesn't change. Over the long term, each utility company in your portfolio will become a solid and significant income producer.

The next step is to create a spreadsheet of industry companies and gather relevant information. Keep it for future reference. This is a 'Process Suggestion' found earlier in the book. Compare company metrics within the industry to determine your next dividend investment candidate.

Appendix B

Summary of Rules

Rule 1: If you are not concerned about your money, don't expect anyone else to be.

Rule 2: Adopt solid investment processes, and use them over and over.

Rule 3: Set financial goals and work to achieve them.

Rule 4: Learn financial terminology. Be able to understand what is being said on business network programs.

Rule 5: The Income Investor should view savings accounts as temporary holding bins to accumulate funds for future investments.

Rule 6: Take a few minutes every month to survey current CD rates. Have a familiarity with the current yield curve. You will be more knowledgeable when you go to the bank to purchase a CD.

Rule 7: Create a portfolio of dividend-producing stocks that produce a reliable, consistent, and growing income stream.

Rule 8: Read at least one analyst report before purchasing a stock.

Rule 9: Have a stock screener method in place so that a large number of stocks can be easily and quickly evaluated using selection criteria. Refine the criteria over time.

Rule 10. Focus on specific industries rather than a shotgun approach across the entire stock market.

Rule 11. Track every dividend payment in a spreadsheet.

Rule 12. Set dividend income goals at the beginning of the year. Periodically compare goal objectives to actual results.

Rule 13: Do not make collective funds part of the income-producing process. Use them for long-term wealth building.

Rule 14: Understand the difference between wealth-building and income-growing.

Rule 15: Blend income production between fixed-income securities and dividend-producing stocks.

Rule 16: Branch out to additional industries over time.

Rule 17: Diversify your industry stock portfolio. And always follow best purchase practices.

Rule 18: Monitor stocks quarterly when the dividend is paid.   Be sensitive to changes in the dividend payment amount. Take appropriate action.

Appendix C

Dividend Goal Calculation

Establishing quarterly dividend income goals involves three elements:

- Goals for the new year are based on the actual fourth-quarter dividends received in the previous year.

- Dividends across your portfolio will naturally increase in the new year by about 4%. This is because your carefully chosen stocks will increase their dividends in the new year. I call this the 'Natural Dividend Growth Goal.'

- The additional amount of quarter-over-quarter dividend growth you want to achieve. I call this the 'Personal Dividend Growth Goal.'

Example

Assume that the total fourth quarter dividends received were $1,000. This is the baseline for the next year.

The Natural Dividend Growth Goal is 4% of $1,000, which equals $40. This is to be allocated over the four quarters in the new year. Therefore, the quarterly income growth goal is $10.

In this example, the Income Investor wants to increase dividend income by $20 each quarter.

Given this information, the following are the quarterly dividend income goals to enter at the bottom of your dividend tracking spreadsheet:

First Quarter

$1,000 plus $10 + $20 = $1,030

Second Quarter

$1,030 plus $10 + $20 = $1,060

Third Quarter

$1,060 plus $10 + $20 = $1,090

Fourth Quarter

$1,090 plus $10 + $20 = $1,120

Working Backwards

The question for the Income Investor is: How much has to be invested to increase dividend income by $20? This can be calculated using the current price of the stock and the current quarterly dividend per share.

Example

Assume the stock being considered has a $50 share price and pays a quarterly dividend of $.75. This means that the yearly dividend is $3, which equates to a dividend yield of 6%.

Dividing the goal of $20 by the quarterly dividend of $.75, results in 26.7 shares to be purchased. As the current price of the stock is $50 per share, then the required investment is 26.7 times $50, which is $1,335.

www.ingramcontent.com/pod-product-compliance
Lightning Source LLC
Chambersburg PA
CBHW070801290526
45795CB00002B/592